STARTERS

MEDIEVAL CASTLE

Illustrated by
Tanja Komadina

SCRIBBLERS

This edition published MMXVIII by Scribblers,
an imprint of The Salariya Book Company Ltd
25 Marlborough Place,
Brighton BN1 1UB
www.salariya.com

PB ISBN-13: 978-1-912006-91-5

1 3 5 7 9 8 6 4 2

A CIP catalogue record for this book is available from the British Library.

Printed and bound in Malaysia.

Printed on paper from sustainable sources.

Visit
www.salariya.com
for our online catalogue and
free fun stuff.

Contents

Introduction

There were many wars in Europe during the Middle Ages, the period between about AD 1000 and 1450. Hundreds of castles were built as protection against enemy armies and as homes for lords and their followers. From these castle strongholds, warrior kings and barons could command and control the lands they ruled.

The first castles, called 'motte and bailey', were built around 1070. They were made of wood. The tower was built on top of a mound (motte). Below that was the bailey – a fenced area to protect the other buildings.

In later years castles were rebuilt in stone. By the 12th century, the stone keep (the central tower) would have been protected by stone walls called curtain walls.

By the 1300s castles were much bigger. They now had a second curtain wall and a gatehouse. These castles were like fortresses. They were almost completely safe from attack.

On each spread you will have to look for different objects in the main picture.

Can you find...?

Castle Design

Castle sites were chosen carefully – sometimes on steep hills (making it easier to defend the castle), or beside important road routes (making it easier to control trade). The castle was ruled by a king or lord, but many poorer people (such as farmers or soldiers) lived and worked in or around castles.

▲Farms
There were buildings inside the castle walls and farms outside. These were usually the first target for any attackers.

▲The peasants
The castle relied on peasants (poor working people) to grow crops, keep animals for food and to do other important jobs.

▲Knights
Knights vowed to protect their lord. There were also regular soldiers called men-in-arms. They protected the castle.

◀Horses
Horses were shoed and looked after in the stables. How many horses can you see?

◀Hiding from danger

When the castle was under attack, people living nearby could hide safely within the castle walls.

▲Keep

The keep was in the middle of a castle. It was where the lord of the castle lived, along with some of his more important subjects.

▲Moat

This was a ditch, filled with water, that surrounded the castle. It was to keep attackers out. The drawbridge was the only way to cross it.

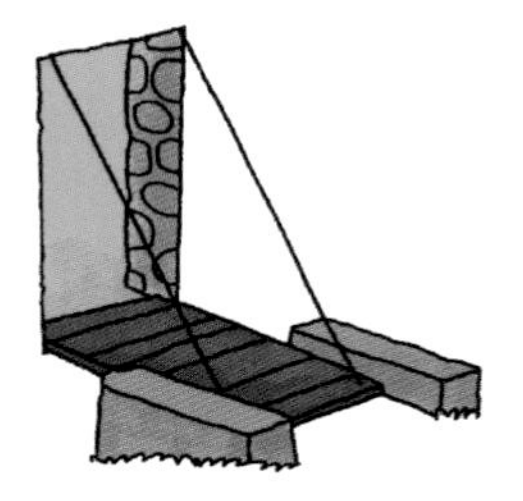

▲Drawbridge

The drawbridge could be pulled up and closed to stop attackers from entering. Can you see the drawbridge in this picture?

▶Gatehouse

The gatehouse was the entry point into the castle. It was a weak spot in its strong walls.

Can you find...?

▲Knights
One of the lord's duties was to choose which squires to make into knights.

▲Musician
Drums, lutes, fiddles or viols were played to entertain guests. Can you find the musicians?

▲Wine
Wine was served in patterned jugs called tankards. Poorer people drank ale or cider.

The Great Hall

The great hall was in the keep, at the centre of the castle. The lord of the castle sat in judgement there every morning to listen to his tenants' problems and to punish criminals. Feasts were held there on special occasions. The most important people got to sit closest to the lord's 'high table'. The main meal of the day, eaten around 10 am, could last for two or three hours.

◀Candles
A candlemaker (or chandler) made the candles out of beeswax.

◀Food

Food served at a feast was meant to show off the lord's wealth. A food taster tested all food before it was eaten.

▲Fireplace

A large fireplace heated the great hall. Can you find the fireplace?

▲Waiter

Food was served to the guests by pages (young boys training to be knights). How many waiters can you count?

▲Jesters

To entertain the guests, jesters would sing, juggle, tell jokes or make fun of people.

◀Hunting Dogs

The lord's dogs were always on the lookout for juicy bones. Can you find the dog with a bone?

The Kitchen

Kitchen servants worked hard making meals for the castle's residents – all two or three hundred of them! They prepared the day-to-day food, as well as the huge feasts in the great hall. Local peasant farmers, called villeins, worked tirelessly rearing animals and harvesting crops to supply food for the castle kitchens. A lot of the farmers' produce was taken by the castle as a form of tax.

◀Workers
The kitchen workers prepared all the food by hand.

Can you find...?

▲Torch
Large torches were hung on walls to light the kitchen. Can you see the torches?

▲Herbs
Herbs like primrose and parsley were often used to add flavour to food.

▲Meat
Meat was salted and stored in large wooden vats to stop it going 'off'.

◀Spit roast
A pig roasted over a fire by turning it on a spit.

▲Flour
Flour was ground in the lord's windmill. Fine flour was used to make white bread for the lord. The servants' brown bread was made with coarse flour.

▲Brick ovens
Brick ovens were outside of the castle in case of fire. Can you see the bread being made?

▲Food
The cooked food was arranged and decorated with great skill to impress the lord's guests.

▶Waiters
Pages and squires (older boys) carried trays of food. How many waiters can you see?

The Keep

In the castle keep was the great hall, the treasury and the chapel. The lord and lady also had a large room there, called the solar, where they lived and slept. By the 1200s, rooms in the keep were heated by open fires. At each corner of the keep was a spiral staircase which climbed in a clockwise direction. This made it more difficult for right-handed attackers to use their swords while climbing the stairs.

Can you find...?

▶Servants

The keep was bustling with servants, all ready to serve their lord and master.

Guarding the keep

Soldiers were stationed around the keep and on the castle walls. How many soldiers can you find?

Bathing

Nobles only bathed about once a month. Servants had to haul buckets of hot water up to the solar.

Keep walls

The keep was well defended by the curtain walls. The keep was designed to withstand attackers.

▲Sleeping quarters

The lord and lady slept in a fine bed. Servants living in the keep had few luxuries. Can you see the lord's bedroom?

Can you find...?

▲Men-at-arms
Men-at-arms often wrestled each other to keep fit.

▲Farrier
The farrier's job of looking after the horses was very important. A warhorse was the most costly thing a knight had to buy. Can you see the farrier?

▲Blacksmith
A blacksmith made lots of things, including weapons, for the castle. His forge was in the bailey. Can you find the forge?

Inside the Castle

The bailey was like a bustling village inside the castle walls. Its residents could supply almost everything the castle needed. This could mean the difference between life or death when under siege. With the enemy surrounding the castle walls, it was the residents of the bailey who supplied the food and skills to keep the castle running.

◀Exercise yard
Men-at-arms trained in the bailey's exercise yard.

▶Cobblers

Cobblers made shoes for the nobles and boots for the soldiers.

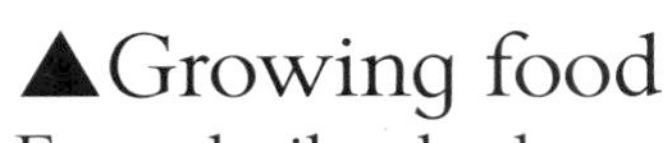

▲Growing food

Every bailey had a small farm with vegetable plots to supply the castle in times of siege. Can you find it?

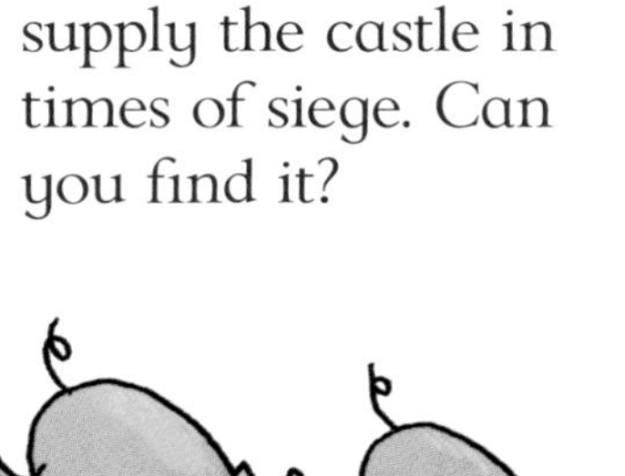

▲Animals

Many of the bailey's farms reared animals to supply the castle with milk, eggs or meat. How many pigs can you see?

▲Bailey residents

The bailey residents were poorer than the lord and his noble friends, but everyone helped to supply and support the castle.

▶Well

Baileys often had a well – a vital water supply in times of siege.

Can you find...?

The Tournament

▲The knight

Knights entered tournaments to practise their fighting skills and to win prizes. How many knights can you see in this picture?

▲Armour

Knights wore special armour for jousting. It was strengthened to withstand the impact of the opponent's lance.

▲Horses

Warhorses were bred to be fearless, to carry knights into battle. Every knight had to have at least two horses. Can you see the horse's armour?

◀Stopping fights

Men-at-arms sometimes had to stop a fight if a knight had cheated.

◀Heraldry

The colours and symbols displayed on shields and flags were used to identify each knight. Can you see this shield?

▲Audience

Many people came to watch tournaments. They became huge social events. Can you see the lord and his nobles?

▲Tent

Knights had their own tents at a tournament for servants, weapons and armour. How many tents can you see in this picture?

Many knights performed in tournaments as practice for warfare. This also allowed them to display their fighting skills and bravery in front of an audience. The most common form of fighting was the joust, where two knights charged at each other on horseback with lances. A joust often meant injury or even death for the loser. For the winner there were rich prizes: they could win armour, money and horses. When knights went to tournaments, they took servants, grooms and squires with them.

▶Squires

Each knight had a squire, who would help him prepare for the tournament. Can you see the squires helping?

Can you find...?

Siege!

▲Mantlet
These large shields were big enough for men to hide behind.

▲Trebuchet
A siege machine that could hurl large stones and missiles at a castle. Can you find the trebuchet?

▲Archer
Sheltered by the castle battlements, archers would shoot at attackers.

Castles were very difficult to attack, and once they were built of stone, it was hard to burn them down. The longer a castle held out against a siege, the worse it would be for its inhabitants if they were captured. Attacking armies often sent messengers into castles to urge them to surrender, or with threats of a dreadful death if they refused to give in.

◀Battering ram

A siege machine used to break through the castle doors or walls. Can you find the battering ram?

▲Soldier on horseback

Soldiers that rode into the attack. How many soldiers on horseback can you see?

▲Siege tower

A siege tower was wheeled right up to the castle walls. Soldiers inside it could then jump onto the battlements.

▲Ladders

Attacking soldiers would also try to climb castle walls using ladders. How many ladders can you see?

▶Foot-soldiers

Soldiers attacking on foot. They were easy targets for archers. How many foot-soldiers can you count?

Timeline

146 BC–AD 476
The Romans built many fortified towns and buildings all over their Empire. Most Roman forts were built to defend the Empire's frontiers.

1080s
The first stone-built keeps were built around the 1100s. These became the strongest part of each castle.

1066
William of Normandy invaded and conquered England. He built a wooden castle at Hastings, which was later rebuilt in stone.

1150–1250s
This was the main period of castle-building in England, France and Germany.

1350

The first castles to be built of brick were in England and the Netherlands.

1530

Castles came to be used as platforms for heavy guns. King Henry VIII built Deal Castle in England for this purpose. It was designed with round, thick, low walls. Many other fortifications along the southern coast of England were used for this purpose.

1400s

Fewer castles were now being built in Europe.

1800

The German fairytale castle of Neuschwanstein was built by King Ludwig of Bavaria.

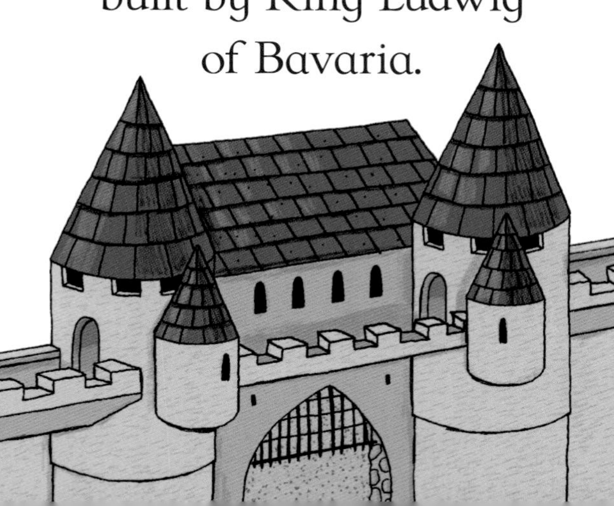

Quiz

1. What is the name of the ditch, filled with water, that surrounds a castle?

2. What do you call the building in the middle of a castle that was home to the lord?

3. What was the food taster's job?

4. Whose job was it to entertain guests at a feast?

5. What was ground in the lord's windmill?

6. What herbs were often used in cooking to add flavour?

7. How often did nobles bathe?

8. Who was in charge of looking after the castle's horses?

9. What was the name of the system of colours and symbols that identified each knight?

10. What powerful weapon could hurl missiles at a castle?

Answers:

1. Moat
2. Keep
3. To test nobles' food
4. Jester
5. Flour
6. Primrose and parsley
7. About once a month
8. The farrier
9. Heraldry
10. Trebuchet

Glossary

Bailey The courtyard of a castle that included stables and other buildings.

Baron A medieval lord who looked after large areas of land for the king.

Battering ram A large wooden tree trunk used to break down castle gates.

Battlements
The parts at the tops of castle walls with square openings for firing arrows through.

Chapel The room used for Christian worship in the keep of a castle.

Lance A weapon used on horseback. It had a long wooden shaft and a metal head.

Medieval A term for the Middle Ages, the period between about AD 1000 and 1450.

Men-at-arms Fully-armed guards who would step in to control tournament fighters with their staffs when necessary.

Siege When an army surrounds the enemy forces in a building or town, cutting off their supplies until they're forced to surrender.

Tax Money or goods that must be given to the ruling power or state.

Treasury The room for storing treasure that belonged to the lord of the castle.

Windmill A building with sails that turn in the wind, rotating a millstone inside. This grinds wheat grains into flour.

Index